UP
UP
IN A
BALLOON

# I Wonder Why

# UP UP UP IN A BALLOON

By Lawrence F. Lowery

Illustrated by Gordon Laite

NSTA Kids
National Science Teachers Association
Arlington, Virginia

## NSTA Kids
### National Science Teachers Association

Claire Reinburg, Director
Jennifer Horak, Managing Editor
Andrew Cooke, Senior Editor
Amanda O'Brien, Associate Editor
Wendy Rubin, Associate Editor
Amy America, Book Acquisitions Coordinator

**ART AND DESIGN**
Will Thomas Jr., Director
Joseph Butera, Cover, Interior Design
Original illustrations by Gordon Laite

**PRINTING AND PRODUCTION**
Catherine Lorrain, Director

**NATIONAL SCIENCE TEACHERS ASSOCIATION**
David L. Evans, Executive Director
David Beacom, Publisher

1840 Wilson Blvd., Arlington, VA 22201
*www.nsta.org/store*
For customer service inquiries, please call 800-277-5300.

Lexile® measure: 620L

*NSTA is committed to publishing material that promotes the best in inquiry-based science education. However, conditions of actual use may vary, and the safety proce-dures and practices described in this book are intended to serve only as a guide. Additional precautionary measures may be required. NSTA and the authors do not war-rant or represent that the procedures and practices in this book meet any safety code or standard of federal, state, or local regulations. NSTA and the authors disclaim any liability for personal injury or damage to property arising out of or relating to the use of this book, including any of the recommendations, instructions, or materials contained therein.*

## PERMISSIONS
Book purchasers may photocopy, print, or e-mail up to five copies of an NSTA book chapter for personal use only; this does not include display or promotional use. Elementary, middle, and high school teachers may reproduce forms, sample documents, and single NSTA book chapters needed for classroom or noncommercial, professional-development use only. E-book buyers may download files to multiple personal devices but are prohibited from posting the files to third-party servers or websites, or from passing files to non-buyers. For additional permission to photocopy or use material electronically from this NSTA Press book, please contact the Copyright Clearance Center (CCC) (*www.copyright.com*; 978-750-8400). Please access *www.nsta.org/permissions* for further information about NSTA's rights and permissions policies.

Library of Congress Cataloging-in-Publication Data
Lowery, Lawrence F.
  Up, up in a balloon : I wonder why / by Lawrence F. Lowery ; illustrated by Gordon Laite.
     pages cm
ISBN 978-1-938946-14-1 (print) -- ISBN 978-1-938946-70-7 (e-book)  1.  Montgolfier, Joseph-Michel, 1740-1810--Juvenile literature.  2.  Montgolfier, Jacques-Etienne, 1745-1799--Juvenile literature.  3.  Balloonists--France--Biography--Juvenile literature.  4.  Ballooning--France--History--18th century--Juvenile literature.  5.  Aeronautics--France--History--18th century--Juvenile literature.  I. Laite, Gordon, illustrator. II. Title.
  TL617.M66L69 2013
  629.13092'244--dc23
                    2013021197

Cataloging-in-Publication Data are also available from the Library of Congress for the e-book.

# Introduction

The *I Wonder Why* books are science books created specifically for young learners who are in their first years of school. The content for each book was chosen to be appropriate for youngsters who are beginning to construct knowledge of the world around them. These youngsters ask questions. They want to know about things. They are more curious than they will be when they are a decade older. Research shows that science is students' favorite subject when they enter school for the first time.

Science is both *what* we know and *how* we come to know it. What we know is the content knowledge that accumulates over time as scientists continue to explore the universe in which we live. How we come to know science is the set of thinking and reasoning processes we use to get answers to the questions and inquiries in which we are engaged.

Scientists learn by observing, comparing, and organizing the objects and ideas they are investigating. Children learn the same way. These thinking processes are among several inquiry behaviors that enable us to find out about our world and how it works. Observing, comparing, and organizing are fundamental to the more advanced thinking processes of relating, experimenting, and inferring.

The five books in this set of the *I Wonder Why* series focus on Earth science content. The materials of our Earth are mostly in the forms of solids (rocks and minerals), liquids (water), and gases (air). Inquiries about these materials are initiated by curiosity. When we don't know something about an area of interest, we try to understand it by asking questions and doing investigations. These five Earth science books are written from the learner's point of view: *How Does the Wind Blow?*; *Clouds, Rain, Clouds Again*; *Spenser and the Rocks*; *Environments of Our Earth*; and *Up, Up in a Balloon*. Children inquire about pebbles and rocks, rain and wind, and jungles and deserts. Their curiosity leads them to ask questions about land forms, weather, and climate.

The information in these books leads the characters and the reader to discover how wind can be measured and how powerful it can be, how the water cycle works, that living things need water to survive, and that plants and animals have adapted to different climate-related environments. They also learn how people have learned to fly in the ocean of air that surrounds Earth.

Each book uses a different approach to take the reader through simple scientific information. One book is expository, providing factual information. Several are narratives that allow a story to unfold. Another provides a historical perspective that tells how we gradually learn science through experimentations over time. The combination of different artwork, literary perspectives, and scientific knowledge brings the content to the reader through several instructional avenues.

In addition, the content in these books correlates to criteria set forth by national standards. Often the content is woven into each book so that its presence is subtle but powerful. The science activities in the Parent/Teacher Handbook section in each book enable learners to carry out their own investigations that relate to the content of the book. The materials needed for these activities are easily obtained, and the activities have been tested with youngsters to be sure they are age appropriate.

After students have completed a science activity, rereading or referring back to the book and talking about connections with the activity can be a deepening experience that stabilizes the learning as a long-term memory.

Many years ago, in a town in France, there lived a man who made paper bags.
He had a wife and two fine sons. The sons were named Joseph and Jacques.

Perhaps the boys read many books about air.
Perhaps they wanted to do something interesting
and important with all those paper bags. Whatever
the reason, when they grew up, the sons began to
experiment with their father's bags.

One day, Joseph and Jacques filled a paper bag with
smoke. They did this without burning the bag or their
hands. They saw that smoke seemed to lift the bag.

Sometime later, Joseph found that it was the heat,
not the smoke, that lifted the bag. Warm air under
the bag made the bag float. "Like a cork floating on
water," thought Joseph. Or maybe it was Jacques.

So hour after hour, the two brothers tried different ways to warm air. "But don't burn the balloon," said Jacques. Or maybe Joseph said that. By then, the brothers thought of the paper bags as balloons.

To heat the air, Joseph would carefully burn bits of wood and straw. Jacques would hold the paper balloons over the fire. Then they would change places.

When the air became warm enough and the balloon had enough of the warm air, the balloon would lift up from the ground and begin to float away.

"Great!" shouted Jacques each time.

"Terrific!" agreed Joseph.

Though sometimes Joseph said, "Great!" and Jacques said, "Terrific!"

Because of the floating balloons, Joseph and Jacques became famous. Everyone in the town was interested in what they were doing.

The two brothers built a gigantic paper balloon.
Then they invited many other people from their
town and other towns to a demonstration of their
wonderful invention.

Joseph and Jacques built a large fire underneath, but not touching, the giant balloon. The fire warmed the air, and the warm air began to fill the balloon.

To the surprise and delight of the invited guests, the balloon began to rise and float away. Up, up it went. Higher and higher it climbed into the sky.

How the people cheered. "Great!" some of them exclaimed. Others said, "Terrific!" The two brothers had invented a flying balloon!

In those days, no one had ever heard of an airplane. No one had even started to invent one. So you can imagine how excited people were about a flying balloon.

The visitors went back to their own towns. They told everybody what they had seen. People all over became interested in balloons.

You would think that everyone would have wanted to go for a ride in the balloon. Not true! People were frightened at the idea of riding in a paper balloon. "The paper might tear, and down we would come with a crash," said one person. "The air would cool and that would make the balloon fall," said another.

Some people felt it would be safer if the balloons were made of cloth. Cloth, after all, was stronger than paper.

Other people thought it would be safer if the air did not need to be heated. No one would have to worry about the air cooling off and the balloon falling.

Around this time, a gas lighter than air was discovered. The name of the gas was hydrogen. Hydrogen was just the right thing for a balloon. It did not have to be heated. It rose above air naturally.

Back in their town, Joseph and Jacques may or may not have heard of the gas. If they did, Joseph probably said, "Great!" and Jacques, "Terrific!"—unless Jacques said, "Great!" and Joseph, "Terrific!"

**Hydrogen can escape between threads in cloth**

**Rubber fills up holes between threads**

Someone made a balloon out of cloth and filled it with hydrogen gas. Up it went—but not for long. The cloth leaked! Gas came out through tiny holes in the cloth. Perhaps no one would ever get to ride in a lighter-than-air balloon!

Then someone thought of rubber. If they put a thin coat of rubber on a cloth balloon, the holes in the cloth would be plugged. This would stop the gas from leaking out of the balloon. Perhaps someone would get to ride in a lighter-than-air balloon after all!

A large, rubber-coated balloon was made and filled
with hydrogen gas. Another demonstration was held.
Hundreds of people waited to see what would happen.
Joseph and Jacques were there too.

FIRST HYDROGEN BALLOON TRIP
AUGUST 27, 1783

As soon as the balloon was released, up into the sky it went. It floated to a height of 3,000 feet.

As the people watched, it began to rain. Would the rain stop the balloon? No! Higher and higher the balloon climbed. Up through the clouds it floated.

"I'm getting wet," announced Jacques. Or maybe it was Joseph. No one heard him. People were so interested in watching this wonderful event that they did not notice how wet they were getting.

The strangest thing about this event had yet to happen. About an hour had passed when, suddenly, a small tear appeared in the cloth. The hydrogen gas began to leak out of the balloon. The balloon began to come back down to the ground, far away from the crowd.

A group of farmers who had not heard about balloons saw the balloon coming down from the clouds. They thought the huge, round thing was a monster. "After it!" shouted one farmer. "After it!" joined in the others.

One farmer shot the balloon with his gun. Other farmers attacked the great rubber-coated, cloth bag with their pitchforks. They tore it to pieces. For good measure, they tied the pieces to a horse's tail and had the horse drag the pieces all over the countryside.

The people who had made the balloon were very unhappy. Something had to be done to let the farmers know about flying balloons. Balloons were not monsters! Balloons could not attack anybody!

So notices were put up to tell people about the wonderful new invention.

Meanwhile, Joseph was invited by the king to demonstrate a hydrogen balloon. Jacques helped him. Both were excited.

"Great!"

"Terrific!"

LOUIS XVI - KING OF FRANCE AND MARIE ANTOINETTE QUEEN

19 SEPTEMBER 1783

The king watched Joseph put three animals in a cage attached to the balloon—a duck, a rooster, and a sheep.

The animals had a safe ride. They were carried more than 1,000 feet into the air. In about 8 minutes, they traveled nearly 2 miles.

So three farm animals were the first air travelers.

The king was impressed. He thought that people could also be sent up into the air. However, no one wanted to go. So the king decided to send two prisoners.

That upset one of the king's friends. That man did not think the honor of being the first person to fly in the air should be given to prisoners. He felt, too, that it was not fair to the prisoners because they had not had a choice.

The friend decided to go himself.

Pilatre de Rozier

FIRST MAN IN SPACE

When all was ready, up went the hot air balloon. The friend found that he could stay up in the air for as long as the air in the balloon remained warm.

Although the trip took him only 84 feet into the air, he won the honor of being the very first person to fly in the air.

Because of that flight, other people became braver. Soon, more great flying balloons floated across the sky. Sometimes they carried several passengers. Sometimes they carried only one person who wanted to be alone in the clouds.

Joseph and Jacques and their paper balloons were the first step toward the many flights we now take in space.

# Parent/Teacher Handbook

## Introduction

*Up, Up in a Balloon* is about the pioneering efforts of the Montgolfier brothers, Joseph and Jacques, and others who tested and sent up balloons in an attempt to help people fly.

## Inquiry Processes

The historical account of the first flight is a good illustration of scientific processes in action. Repeated testing of various materials, new means of gas production, trials of different kinds of gases, and the solution of technical problems such as gas leaks are all typical actions in working toward a solution to any problem. The test and retest processes are threaded throughout this story to give the reader a sense of science in action.

## Content

The experimentation of the Montgolfier brothers and others is related in a simple fashion. From their earliest experiments, the brothers learned it was possible to produce enough lift to overcome the force of gravity. A balloon floats because of the upward push or buoyant force of the air on the balloon; if the buoyant force of the air is greater than the weight of the balloon, then the balloon rises.

The reader will note various stages in balloon flight testing. Use of cloth balloons, attempts with rubber-coated cloth balloons, and trials with hydrogen rather than warm air were stages in the improvement of the flight device itself. The factory tests with paper bags, the flight that carried animals, and the attempt to force prisoners to become the first people to fly were stages in the progress of flight. Actually, a Frenchman named Pilatre de Rozier volunteered in place of the prisoners and became the first man to fly, on October 15, 1783.

Events in this story actually happened. Farmers were frightened by early balloons. The king demanded to see a test. All the beautiful balloons in the illustrations were based on the actual balloons used in the early flight tests. The dialogue, however, was made up to move the story along.

# Science Activities

## Seeing the Effect of Warm Air in a Paper Bag

Suspend an inverted empty bag at each end of a stick that is balanced at a point in the center of the stick. Heat the air under one bag with a lighted light bulb. Observe what happens after one bag is filled with warm air and the other stays cooler at room temperature.

## Observing That Warmer Air Seems to Be Above Cooler Air

Use a thermometer to measure the temperature of the air at various heights in a room. Take the temperature in different rooms.

Warm air is lighter than cooler air. The cooler air pushes the warm air out of its way, making the warm air seem to rise upward. The hot air will gather at the highest points near the ceiling.

## Observing That Air Moving Rapidly Across the Top Surface of a Wing Causes It to Lift

Place a 2 in. × 10 in. (5 cm × 25 cm) strip of paper between the pages of a book standing upright so the paper hangs out over the top. Use a straw with a large diameter to blow a stream of air across the top surface of the piece of paper. (The paper will rise.)

Fasten a paper clip to the end of the paper strip and blow again. Repeat to see how many paper clips can be lifted by a stream of air.

When air moves rapidly, it is accompanied by a decrease in air pressure. Because the decrease on the top side of the paper is less than on the lower side, the greater air pressure underneath pushes the paper upward.

## Experimenting to See What Effect Differently Shaped Wings Have on Flight

Experiment with the wing design of paper gliders. Test broad, narrow, or differently shaped wings to see how well each provides lift for the craft. The following shows how to make broad-wing and narrow-wing gliders for testing.

### Narrow-Wing Glider

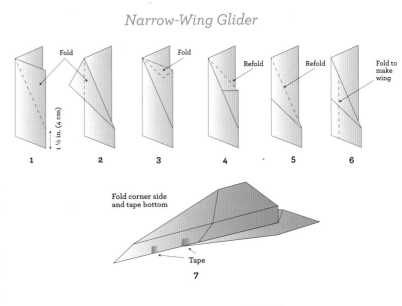

### Broad-Wing Glider

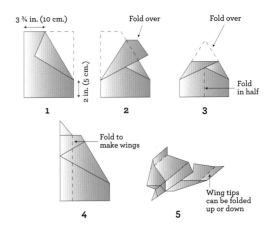

Now create some gliders of your own design.

*Another activity can be found at* www.nsta.org/balloon.